J. D.
VANCE

J. D. VANCE

From Rural America to the White House

Matt Doeden

LERNER PUBLICATIONS ◆ MINNEAPOLIS

Lerner Publications Company
An imprint of Lerner Publishing Group, Inc.
241 First Avenue North
Minneapolis, MN 55401 USA

For reading levels and more information, look up this title at www.lernerbooks.com.

Main body text set in Rotis Serif Std 55 Regular. Typeface provided by Adobe Systems.

Library of Congress Cataloging-in-Publication Data

Names: Doeden, Matt, author.
Title: J.D. Vance : from rural America to the White House / Matt Doeden.
Description: Lerner Publications Minneapolis : Lerner Publications, [2025] | Series: Gateway biographies | Includes bibliographical references and index. | Audience: Ages 9–14 | Audience: Grades 4–6 | Summary: "In 2024 US voters chose their next president and vice president. The vice president fulfills many important roles in the US government. They serve as the president's backup and also preside over the Senate."– Provided by publisher.
Identifiers: LCCN 2024041488 (print) | LCCN 2024041489 (ebook) | ISBN 9798765649176 (library binding) | ISBN 9798765661826 (paperback) | ISBN 9798765654873 (epub)
Subjects: LCSH: Vance, J. D.—Juvenile literature. | Politicians—Ohio—Biography—Juvenile literature. | United States. Congress. Senate—Biography—Juvenile literature. | Vice-presidents—United States—Election—2024—Juvenile literature. | Ohio—Biography—Juvenile literature.
Classification: LCC E901.1.V36 D64 2025 (print) | LCC E901.1.V36 (ebook) | DDC 328.73/092—dc23/eng/20240905

LC record available at https://lccn.loc.gov/2024041488
LC ebook record available at https://lccn.loc.gov/2024041489

Manufactured in the United States of America
1-1011063-53497-11/12/2024

TABLE OF CONTENTS

Republican vice presidential candidate J. D. Vance at a campaign rally in Radford, Virginia, in July 2024

Nothing had been normal about the 2024 US presidential election. Republican Donald Trump was challenging Democrat Joe Biden in a race to become the next US president. The race was charged with emotions. Republicans accused Biden of being weak. Democrats called Trump a dangerous candidate.

Things got even stranger on July 13, 2024. Trump was speaking at a rally in Pennsylvania when a shooter tried to kill him. The shooter's bullet grazed Trump's ear. Trump, who had been president from 2017 to 2021, escaped death by inches.

Trump speaking at the rally in Pennsylvania prior to getting shot in the ear

Two days later, the Republican National Convention (RNC) began in Milwaukee, Wisconsin. There was no doubt who the Republican candidate for president would be. It was Trump. But no one knew who he would pick as his running mate. Many expected it to be a well-known politician such as Florida Senator Marco Rubio.

But Trump had never been one to do the expected. He didn't pick a household name. He didn't choose an experienced politician. "After lengthy deliberation . . . I have decided that the person best suited to assume the position of Vice President of the United States is Senator J. D. Vance of the Great State of Ohio," Trump wrote on social media.

It was a surprising choice. Vance had once been a big critic of Trump. He had spoken out against Trump during his 2016 presidential campaign. Vance also didn't have a long history in government. He had little name recognition outside of Ohio. But he was young and energetic, with a military background. Republicans hoped he could bring fresh life into the campaign.

Two days after Trump chose Vance, the thirty-nine-year-old Ohio senator took the stage at the RNC in Milwaukee. The crowd of supporters roared as the newest rising star in American politics introduced himself to the nation. He spoke about growing up in a small town and his struggles to overcome a challenging upbringing.

Vance points toward the crowd at the 2024 RNC.

"Some people tell me I've lived the American dream, and of course, they're right, and I'm so grateful for it," he said. "But the American dream that has always counted most was not starting a business or becoming a senator or even being here. . . . My most important American dream was becoming a good husband and a good dad. . . . I wanted to give my kids the things that I didn't have when I was growing up, and that's the accomplishment I'm proudest of."

As the crowd cheered, there was no doubt that hardcore Republicans supported Vance. But would he appeal to other voters? Every candidate faces lots of criticism. Everything they've ever done or said is analyzed. Would Vance stand up to the criticism?

Vance on the third day of the 2024 RNC

Vance grew up in Middletown, Ohio, which had a population of around 43,000 in the 1980s.

Rough Childhood

James Donald Bowman was born on August 2, 1984, in Middletown, Ohio. Life for young J. D. was complicated. His father, Donald Bowman, left the family when J. D. was just a toddler. His mother, Beverly Vance, married Bob Hamel, who adopted J. D. She didn't want her son named for Donald Bowman anymore, so she changed J. D.'s name to James David Hamel after her husband and one of J. D.'s uncles. J. D. lived with the couple and his older sister, Lindsay. Hamel didn't stay in their lives for very long, but J. D. remembered him as a kind man.

Life was changing. But it wasn't getting any easier for little J. D. His mom struggled with drug addiction. She didn't take good care of her son. The family moved constantly. J. D. recalled a day when he was about eleven years old. He was in the car with his mother. Something he'd said angered her. She stepped on the car's accelerator, speeding up more and more. She told J. D. that she was going to crash the car and kill them both. When she finally slowed down, she turned and hit her son. J. D. jumped out of the car and ran to a stranger's house to call the police.

It was a hard way to grow up. J. D. said that some days he was grateful just to have survived another day. But as bad as things were with his mother, J. D. had one source of stability in his life. He spent lots of time with his grandparents, James and Bonnie Vance. Though they did not live there anymore, J. D. would often visit his grandparents' hometown of Jackson,

J. D.'s family comes from Jackson, Kentucky. His grandparents moved to Ohio when they were young to find better-paying jobs.

Kentucky. It soon became clear that Beverly couldn't raise her children responsibly, so the Vances began looking after them.

"In Ohio, I was the abandoned son of a man I hardly knew and a woman I wished I didn't," J. D. wrote. "In Jackson, I was the grandson of the toughest woman anyone knew and the most skilled auto mechanic in town."

The Vances raised the kids. But J. D.'s relationship with his parents remained rocky. Bowman briefly came back into his life the summer J. D. turned eleven. But the two never made much of a connection.

From High School to the Marines

J. D. attended Middletown High School. It was a tough environment. Middletown was not a wealthy town. The school didn't have a lot of resources. Many of the students didn't take education seriously. At times in his life, J. D. was among them. By the time he was in ninth grade, his grades had him on the verge of flunking out of school. He was absent all the time. He began to experiment with alcohol and drugs.

"I was one of those kids with a grim future," he wrote. "I almost failed out of high school. I nearly gave in to the deep anger and resentment harbored by everyone around me. . . . Whatever talents I have, I almost squandered until a handful of loving people rescued me."

The Rust Belt

J. D. spent his childhood in a part of the country called the Rust Belt. This area covers parts of the Northeastern and Midwestern United States that was once known as the Steel Belt. It was called that because it had many major steel and manufacturing industries. Its name changed when the region saw a decline in industry—including steel production—which has left parts of this region in bad condition. Many of its people struggle to get by.

Those loving people included his grandmother. Bonnie Vance never graduated from high school, but she strongly valued education. She pushed J. D. to do better. J. D.'s mom also pushed him to do well in school. She made sure J. D. had a library card at an early age. Meanwhile, J. D. felt inspired by one of his high school teachers. This teacher encouraged students in class and sparked their joy in learning. Bonnie Vance told J. D. to follow this teacher's lead and to go to college. But to do that, J. D. would have to put in the work and bring up his grades.

J. D. took school seriously again. His grades improved. He got a job at a local grocery store to earn some money.

J. D. graduated from high school in 2003. He wanted to go to college at Ohio State University, but the tuition was expensive. J. D. and his family had never had much money, and he just couldn't convince himself that it was worth it. He wanted to find another way.

Hitting the Course

In 2002, before his senior year of high school, J. D. became interested in golf. He wanted to join the high school team, so he practiced his swing at home, without using any golf balls. Soon, he took a job at a golf course so he could practice for free. Finally, he tried out for the team. He didn't make it. Most of the other students had been playing for years. It was a disappointment. But he didn't regret trying.

So he did. J. D. talked to a recruiter for the US Marine Corps. The idea of joining the Marine Corps felt almost laughable to him. "I was a pudgy, longhaired kid," he recalled. "When our gym teacher told us to run a mile [1.6 km], I'd walk at least half. I had never woken up before six a.m. And here was this organization promising that I'd rise regularly at five a.m. and run multiple miles per day."

Yet J. D. couldn't get the idea out of his head. The Marine Corps offered a sense of order and stability that had been missing in his life. And serving in the military would open new ways of paying for the education that he wanted. The memory of the attacks of September 11, 2001, was still fresh in his mind. J. D. felt the appeal of serving his country in the battle against terrorism, so he enlisted.

J. D.'s decision surprised almost everyone around him—including himself. By enlisting, he was agreeing to give four years to the Marine Corps. He didn't know what he'd be doing—or where. The Iraq War (2003–2011) had just started. Would he end up there? Would he even make it home alive?

Serving His Country

In 2003 Hamel got on a plane and headed for boot camp at the Marine Corps Recruit Depot in Parris Island, South Carolina. Like all enlisted marines, Hamel was heading into thirteen weeks of intense training.

It was hard for him. He came to boot camp in poor shape. The physical demands wore him down, and the mental stress of just trying to survive each day took its toll. On one of his first days, he took a piece of cake at mealtime. A drill instructor knocked the plate out of his hands and told him that he was too fat for cake. But his grandmother and sister wrote him letters almost every day. He said that their letters helped keep him strong even in the tough times.

Hamel quickly learned that he was capable of more than he'd known. "Every time the drill instructor screamed at me and I stood proudly; every time I thought I'd fall behind during a run and kept up; every time I learned to do something I thought impossible, like climb the rope, I came a little closer to believing in myself," he wrote in his 2016 memoir.

Thirteen weeks after he stepped off the plane, Hamel completed boot camp. His grandmother and other relatives came to watch as he officially became a marine in his graduation ceremony. He called it the proudest day of his life.

Hamel joined the Marine Corps in 2003.

A Marine Corps graduation ceremony in 2024

Hamel was assigned to the Second Marine Aircraft Wing, based in North Carolina. The Marine Corps puts its new members through heavy testing to learn their strengths and weaknesses. Hamel's talent with words earned him a job as a military journalist.

In 2005 Hamel's unit was preparing to go to Iraq. Weeks before he left, his grandmother fell very ill. Hamel rushed home and was able to see her just before she died. He was able to go to her funeral before returning to his unit and heading to a war zone.

Hamel was lucky. He wasn't there to fight. Of course, as a marine he could be called to combat if needed. But his job there was mostly to escort journalists and to take photos and write stories about other marines serving on the front lines. He also worked with civil affairs. That part of the job involved going into the community. He visited Iraqi schools and other locations to meet with the local people. He later recalled meeting Iraqi children who had so little and lived surrounded by violence. It gave him a deep appreciation for his country and its opportunities.

After six months in Iraq, Hamel returned to the United States. He spent time as the media relations officer at Marine Corps Air Station Cherry Point and rose to the rank of corporal. In 2007 his service time was over. He was honorably discharged, or released, from the Marine Corps. Hamel was a changed man. He had entered the Marine Corps as an out-of-shape, angry kid. He left as a man with a more hopeful view of the world and his place in it. He was ready to take on the next challenge in his life.

Higher Education

As a senior in high school, Hamel had wanted to attend Ohio State University (OSU). The cost of college had changed his mind. But as a former marine, he had access to more resources. Hamel took advantage of the GI Bill. It pays for former military members to attend college.

Hamel enrolled at OSU in 2007. He studied political science and philosophy. Political science is the study of politics and government. Philosophy is the study of the nature of thought, reality, and meaning.

The sprawling campus of OSU in Columbus, Ohio

Hamel had gained a strong work ethic in the military. It served him well at OSU. He was a good student and made friends easily, despite being four years older than most of the other first-year students.

The GI Bill took care of most of Hamel's college expenses, but not all of them, so he got a job at the Ohio Statehouse. He worked under a state senator named Bob Schuler. Hamel had grown up learning from his grandparents, who were both Democrats. But Schuler was a Republican. Hamel liked Schuler and agreed with many of his positions on important issues. His political beliefs began to shift more and more to the Republican side.

Throughout college, Hamel had a range of jobs. He worked for a charity that helped children, served as a tutor, and more. Meanwhile, he loaded up his class schedule. He felt as though he was behind because of his four years in the military. He wanted to graduate early to catch up to his peers. With a lot of hard work, he did. Hamel graduated from OSU in August 2009.

Bob Schuler was elected twice as an Ohio state senator.

Hamel already had his next step in mind. He wanted to go to law school. There was a problem though. Most law school programs began in the fall. His graduation came too late for him to enroll that year, so he moved back to live with family in Middletown and worked at a warehouse and other jobs to save money.

Hamel dreamed of going to Yale Law School. It's one of the best law schools in the nation. At first, he didn't even apply there. He didn't think he had a chance to get in. But he found an application online. It didn't take much time to apply, so he decided to give it a shot. In spring 2010, he got a big surprise. Someone from Yale called him. They had accepted him! And the good news got better. They were offering him scholarships that made it something he could afford.

Hamel started classes at Yale in fall 2010. He quickly became friends with a group of classmates. One of his classmates was Usha Chilukuri, the daughter of Indian immigrants. Over time, the two became inseparable. Their friendship grew into a romance.

Hamel was a talented writer. He used that skill at Yale. In 2011 professor and writer Amy Chua encouraged him to write his memoir—a type of autobiography. Hamel started the project alongside his studies. He also wrote for and edited the *Yale Law Journal*, a well-respected, student-run publication.

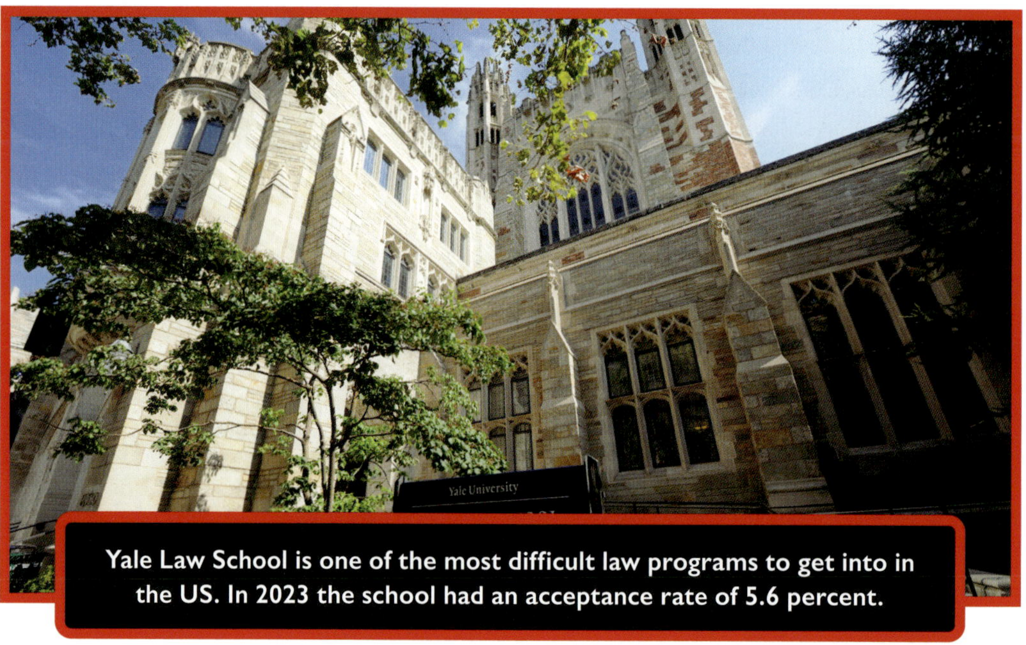

Yale Law School is one of the most difficult law programs to get into in the US. In 2023 the school had an acceptance rate of 5.6 percent.

It wasn't easy. Many of Hamel's fellow students had come from the nation's top private universities. Some students and professors had a low opinion of people from state schools, such as OSU. At a fancy dinner with a law firm that was looking for future employees, Hamel felt lost. He didn't know what to order, which fork to use, or what the proper manners were. Luckily, Chilukuri was there to coach him.

"For all of the joy [of learning], Yale planted a seed of doubt in my mind about whether I belonged," he wrote. But he worked hard to impress his professors—and mostly succeeded.

Amy Chua is known for writing the bestselling memoir *Battle Hymn of the Tiger Mother.*

Meanwhile, Hamel gave a lot of thought to his name. He still carried the last name of Bob Hamel, who had not been a big part of his life. It didn't feel as if it belonged to him. But his father's name didn't feel right either. So he decided to change it to Vance—the last name of the grandparents who had raised him and helped him escape a life of poverty. The name change became official in 2013. Soon after, J. D. Vance graduated from Yale.

Making His Mark

At twenty-nine, Vance was ready for the next stage of his life. He spent some time working for US Senator John Cornyn. Then he and Chilukuri moved to Kentucky, where they both took jobs as clerks for judges. Clerks do legal research, write summaries, handle paperwork, and do other jobs for a judge.

In 2014 Vance and Chilukuri married. He is a Christian. She is a Hindu. So their wedding included traditions from both religions. The couple went on to have three children: Ewan in 2017, Vivek in 2020, and Mirabel in 2021.

Vance with his wife, Usha

Meanwhile, Vance had continued work on the memoir he had started at Yale. In 2016 HarperCollins published it. The book, titled *Hillbilly Elegy: A Memoir of a Family and Culture in Crisis*, tracked the lives of Vance and his family. He went into great detail about his struggles to find a father figure, his frustration with his mom's addiction, and his love for the stability that his grandparents gave him.

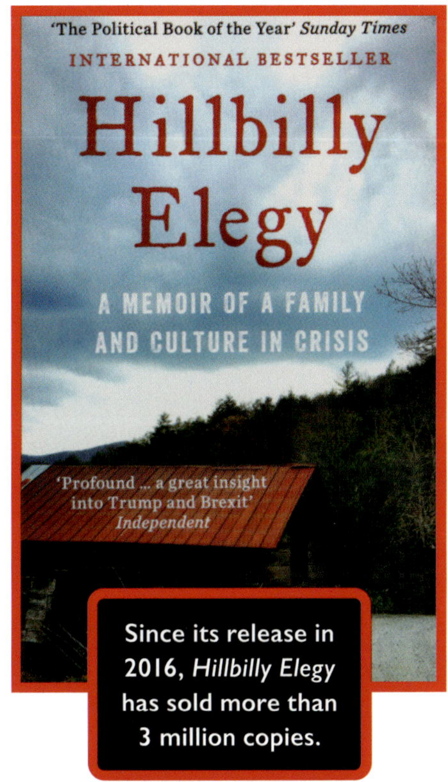

Since its release in 2016, *Hillbilly Elegy* has sold more than 3 million copies.

But the book wasn't just a biography. Vance used it as a way to look at the culture of working-class Americans, especially in the Rust Belt. He wrote about flaws he saw in the American system, from welfare abuse to how people deal with poverty and addiction. He didn't sugarcoat anything. He pointed out flaws in his family, in himself, and in the nation's culture.

People were drawn to his down-to-earth writing style and brutal honesty. It shot onto the *New York Times* bestseller list. Mona Charen of the *National Review* praised Vance's story. "Vance has risen out of chaos to the heights of stability, success, and happiness," she wrote. "He is fundamentally optimistic about the chances for the

From Book to Film

In 2017 a film studio called Imagine Entertainment bought the rights to turn *Hillbilly Elegy* into a film. Award-winning director Ron Howard directed the film, which streamed on Netflix. It featured popular actors Glenn Close (as Bonnie Vance) and Amy Adams (as Beverly Vance). Gabriel Basso played the role of J. D.

The film gained a wide audience and enjoyed some popularity. Close earned an Academy Award nomination for her role. But the film fared poorly with critics. They said it misrepresented Appalachia, the area where Vance is from, and glorified his rise from poverty.

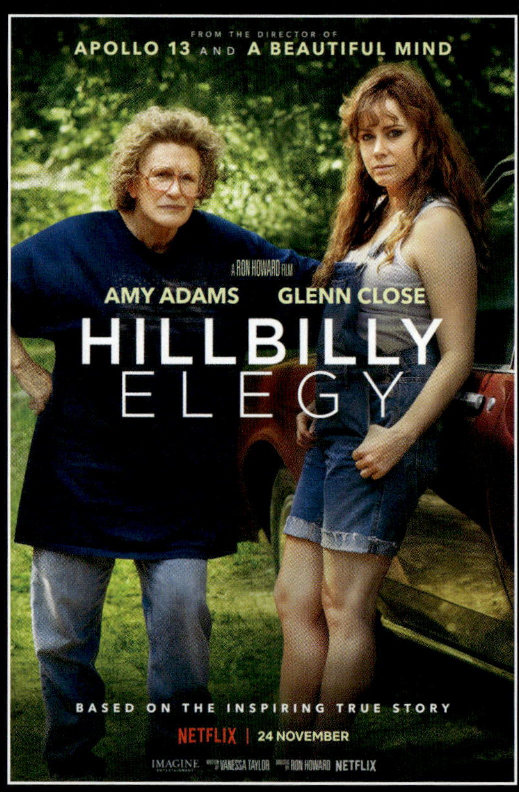

Republican nominee Donald Trump faces Democratic nominee Hillary Clinton in a presidential debate in 2016.

nation to do the same. Whether his optimism is justified or not is unknowable, but his brilliant book is a signal flashing danger."

Of course, not everyone agreed. Critics of the book argued that Vance simplified complex issues. They accused him of patting himself on the back too much. "*Elegy* is little more than a list of myths about welfare queens repackaged as a primer on the white working class," wrote Sarah Jones of the *New Republic*.

Vance's book came out during a time of political change in the United States. Republicans had nominated Donald Trump for president. He was facing Democratic nominee Hillary Clinton in a tight race. Trump was a brash, outspoken outsider with very little political background. Most people knew him as a famous business executive and television personality. Now in politics,

Trump thrived on insulting his opponents—or anyone else he didn't like. Some people loved his style. They felt that he spoke for hardworking Americans.

Others couldn't stand Trump. Vance was among them. As the popularity of his book soared, Vance did interviews and wrote articles about Trump and the election. And he didn't make it a secret how he felt.

"I can't stomach Trump," he said in an interview. "I think that he's noxious and is leading the white working class to a very dark place." Vance became an outspoken member of part of the Republican Party that some called Never Trumpers. This group was strongly against Trump becoming president.

Vance's public profile was on the rise. In 2015 he and Usha moved to San Francisco, California. Vance joined a company called Mithril Capital. The group invested in companies and helped them grow. A year later, he began working for the CNN television network to cover politics.

Running for Office

In 2017 Vance returned to Ohio. He started a nonprofit organization called Our Ohio Renewal. The group aimed to work on issues such as education and support for those living with addiction. Vance hoped the group could make a positive change, but it achieved little over the next few years. Vance also worked with a startup agriculture company called AppHarvest. The company was troubled

Vance speaks at TechCrunch Disrupt, a large tech industry news event, in 2018.

from the start. Employees reported terrible working conditions. AppHarvest went out of business just a few years later.

In 2018 Ohio Democrat Sherrod Brown was up for reelection for the US Senate. Vance thought about running against Brown, but he decided against it. Still, the idea of running for office stuck with him. Three years later, he decided to go for it. Vance announced his plan to run for an open Senate seat on July 1, 2021. His first task was to win the Republican nomination. He took on a crowded field of candidates to win 32 percent of the vote—more than anyone else.

Next came the general election. Vance faced Democrat Tim Ryan, who had served in the US House of Representatives. Vance entered the election as a

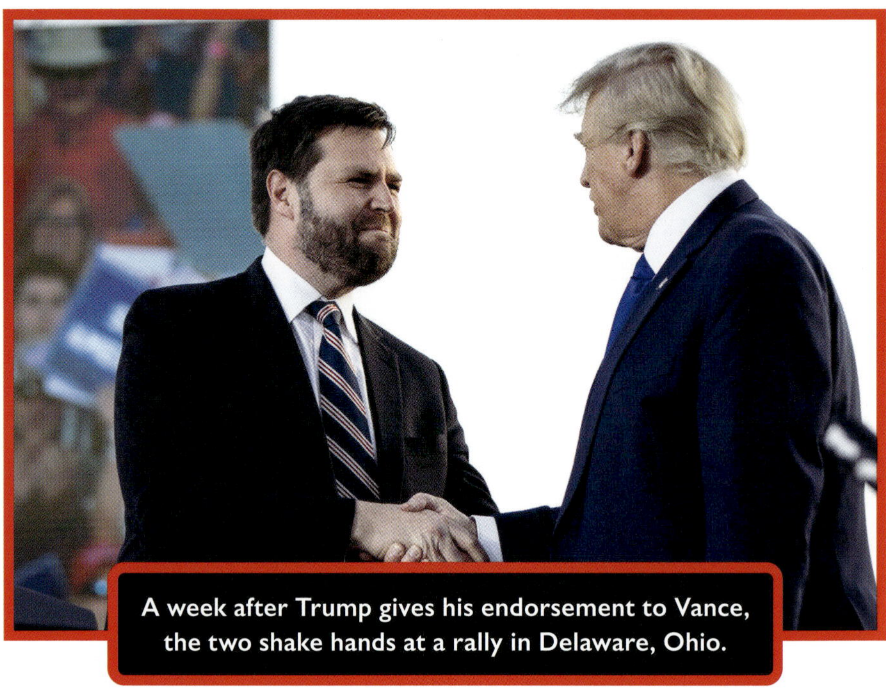

A week after Trump gives his endorsement to Vance, the two shake hands at a rally in Delaware, Ohio.

heavy favorite. Ohio had been leaning more and more Republican in recent years. Trump remained a powerful figure in the Republican Party, so Vance began to change his tune and sing Trump's praises. He earned the former president's endorsement, or backing.

"Like some others, J. D. Vance may have said some not-so-great things about me in the past, but he gets it now, and I have seen that in spades," Trump said. "He is our best chance for victory in what could be a very tough race."

Trump's endorsement was a big deal, but it also opened up Vance to criticism. His opponents accused Vance of kissing up to Trump to gain power. They pointed to his earlier comments on Trump and said that Vance would say anything to get ahead.

Vance hit the campaign trail. He vowed to pass laws to lower taxes and improve the economy. He promised to fight to make abortions illegal. And he spoke against laws and rules that forced people to get vaccines for the COVID-19 pandemic.

The race was much closer than anyone expected. Even up to election day, November 8, 2022, the polls were tight. But as the votes came in, Vance slowly pulled ahead. Late that night, it was clear—Vance was the winner. Ryan called to congratulate him, and the party was on.

The gap between Vance's and Ryan's votes grows on election night. Vance ends the night pulling ahead with about 53 percent of the vote.

Vance speaks to his supporters at a rally on election night.

During a party to celebrate his victory, Vance stepped up to speak to his supporters. "We need better leadership in Washington DC and that's exactly what I promise to fight for every single day," he said. "We have a very simple job to do. It's to go to work every single day and fight for the people of Ohio, fight for our workers."

Senator Vance

Vance was officially sworn in as a US senator on January 3, 2023. Mostly, he worked with Republicans and voted along party lines. But he also worked with the other side. He teamed up with Senator Raphael Gamaliel Warnock, a Democrat from Georgia, and others to cosponsor a bill that would limit the price of the drug insulin. Millions of people with diabetes need the drug, and prices have risen sharply in recent years.

Vance also broke with most Republicans after a train derailed in Ohio, spilling toxic chemicals. He supported using federal funds to help people affected by the spill. Most other Republicans opposed that idea.

Committee assignments are a big part of a senator's job. Committees look into specific issues in depth. During his first years in the Senate, Vance served on a few different committees. They included the Senate Committee on Banking, Housing, and Urban Affairs; the Senate Committee on Commerce, Science, and Transportation; and the Senate Special Committee on Aging.

Vance's official Senate portrait

As the 2024 elections neared, Vance wasn't a name that jumped out to most people. He wasn't up for reelection.

Vance speaks during a Senate hearing on improving rail safety in March 2023.

Senators serve six-year terms. He was a first-term senator who had only been in office less than a year. He had some fame because of the success of his book and his time on CNN. But few considered him a candidate for vice president.

When Trump won the presidency in 2016, Mike Pence was his running mate. For most of his time in office, the two seemed to get along. But that changed when Trump lost to Joe Biden in a tight 2020 race. Trump refused to admit defeat. He accused Biden and Democrats of stealing the election. Trump had no evidence, but that didn't slow down his accusations. Trump told Pence to refuse to certify, or make official, the election results.

Pence didn't like that Biden had won. But he valued democracy. He ignored Trump and certified the election anyway. Trump was furious. Extreme Republicans called Pence a traitor. Some called for him to be killed.

Understanding the Sides

Republicans and Democrats. Conservatives and liberals. Red states and blue states. What does it all mean? The United States has a two-party system. That means two political parties dominate. Republicans—or conservatives—generally favor smaller government and a return to traditional ways. Democrats, sometimes called liberals, tend to favor more government programs to help citizens, with an outlook that chooses progress over tradition. States that usually vote Republican are called red states. Democrat-leaning states are called blue states.

Trump did little to quiet the outrage. So when Trump won the Republican nomination in 2024, he needed a new running mate. As the 2024 RNC approached, political experts buzzed about who Trump might nominate for vice president. Some thought Trump might pick a longtime politician. According to reports, he was ready to choose North Dakota Governor Doug Burgum. But soon before the RNC, he met with his two older sons. They begged him to choose a younger, more exciting candidate. And Vance was the one they had in mind.

They convinced Trump. Two days after a bullet almost took the former president's life, Trump announced his choice. Just like that, Vance became a household name.

Trump with his vice presidential pick, J. D. Vance, on Day 1 of the 2024 RNC

Supporters argued that he was the perfect choice. Trump was seventy-eight years old. At the time, he was running against eighty-one-year-old Biden. Many voters felt it was time for a new generation of leaders. Vance brought youth and energy to the campaign. His military background showed strength and patriotism. He was a good speaker and could get Trump's message across.

But the choice came with huge risks. He'd only spent a year and a half in the US Senate. He'd never held any other political office. He had survived a race for the Senate. But the pressure of running for the White House was a whole new level. Would he rise to expectations?

The Run for the White House

Vance had been thrust into the spotlight. His start on the campaign trail came with ups and downs. He was a big hit at the RNC. A packed arena roared their approval as he spoke—introducing himself to much of the nation.

But it wasn't all smooth sailing. Everything a candidate for vice president says and does is fair game for critics. A comment Vance made in 2021 went viral. He called Democratic leaders "a bunch of childless cat ladies" and said they were "miserable at their own lives and the choices that they've made and so they want to make the rest of the country miserable too." He said that people without children don't have any stake in the future of the country.

Supporters cheer on Vance as he steps into the role of Republican vice presidential nominee.

Vance could have done damage control and backed away from the comment. But he didn't. When asked about it, Vance shrugged it off. He said that it was a bad idea to let people without children decide the future of the country.

It had already been a strange election. But it got even weirder on July 21, 2024, when Biden stepped down from the race. After a bad debate performance where he seemed to struggle to organize his thoughts, pressure had grown on the president to bow out. Republican and Democratic politicians, alongside large donors who gave money to his campaign, urged him to leave the race. He finally agreed. Vice President Kamala Harris stepped in as the new Democratic candidate. Later, she chose Minnesota Governor Tim Walz as her running mate.

Vance's biggest moment in the election came on October 1, 2024. He took on Walz in the vice-presidential debate in New York City. It's the one day in the election where the candidates for vice president are front and center.

A few weeks earlier, Trump and Harris had engaged in a tense debate. Trump had performed poorly, even according to many of his supporters. So Vance really wanted to project a sense of calm and control. Early on, it was clear that Vance was more comfortable onstage. Walz, a former teacher, had admitted that debating wasn't one of his strengths. Unlike Trump and Harris in the presidential debate, the vice presidential candidates were open and friendly with each other. While

CBS News hosts the vice-presidential debate between Vance and Democrat Tim Walz (*second from right*) on October 1, 2024.

Vance's main job was to build up Trump, he also took time to find common ground with Walz.

Vance promised that if he and Trump won, families would be their first priority: "My party, we've got to do so much better of a job at earning the American people's trust back on [reproductive freedom]. . . . I want us, as a Republican Party, to be pro-family in the fullest sense of the word. I want us to support fertility treatments. I want us to make it easier for moms to afford to have babies. I want us to make it easier for young families to afford a home, so they can afford a place to raise that family."

Youth Movement

Forty-year-old Vance is the third-youngest vice president in US history. The youngest was John C. Breckinridge. He was just thirty-six when he and James Buchanan took office in 1857. Richard Nixon was forty years and eleven days old when he became vice president in 1953. Theodore Roosevelt was the youngest president at forty-two.

By November, the race was very tight. It looked like it would come down to a few swing states—states where the polling numbers were so close that they could go either for Harris or Trump. Trump and Vance campaigned furiously in those states, which included Wisconsin, Michigan, Arizona, Pennsylvania, Georgia, North Carolina, and Nevada. They tried to reach groups such as Latinos that traditionally vote for Democratic candidates.

Election day was November 5. Trump and Vance eagerly watched as the votes were counted. The scales started to tip in their favor when projections said they would win in North Carolina and Georgia. Slowly, they built narrow leads in other key states, including Pennsylvania.

Early on the morning of November 6, it was clear. Trump and Vance had won the election. Harris conceded the race, and Trump spoke to his excited supporters. At one point, Trump invited Vance to speak as well—a rarity for vice presidential candidates. Vance told the crowd how thrilled he was and that their victory was the greatest political comeback story in the history of the country.

After just two years in public office, Vance had climbed all the way to the White House. He and Trump prepared for their term, which was set to begin in January 2025. What does the future hold for Vance? What will Americans think of his leadership? Will he be a candidate for president in 2028? Only time will tell.

IMPORTANT DATES

1984 James Donald Bowman is born on August 2 in Middletown, Ohio.

1985 J. D.'s father leaves the family. His mother later changes J. D.'s name to James David Hamel.

2000 As a first-year student in high school, Hamel nearly flunks out of school.

2003 Hamel graduates from high school and enlists in the Marine Corps.

2005 Hamel's unit is deployed to Iraq. He spends six months there.

2007 Hamel is honorably discharged from the Marine Corps. He enrolls at Ohio State University.

2009 Hamel graduates from OSU with degrees in political science and philosophy.

2010 Hamel enrolls at Yale Law School. He meets Usha Chilukuri.

2011	A professor convinces Hamel to write his memoir.
2013	Hamel changes his name to J. D. Vance and graduates from Yale.
2014	Vance and Chilukuri wed.
2016	HarperCollins publishes Vance's memoir, *Hillbilly Elegy*. It becomes a bestseller.
	Vance is an outspoken critic of Donald Trump during the 2016 election.
2022	Vance wins a close election in Ohio over Tim Ryan to earn a US Senate seat.
2023	Vance is sworn in as a US senator.
2024	In a surprise move, Trump chooses Vance to be his running mate in the presidential election. Vance begins campaigning for the office of vice president.
2025	Vance is sworn in as vice president of the United States.

SOURCE NOTES

8 Alice Herman and Sam Levine, "Trump Names J. D. Vance, Once One of His Fiercest Critics, as 2024 Running Mate," *Guardian* (US edition), July 15, 2024, https://www.theguardian.com/us-news/article/2024/jul/15/trump-vp-jd-vance-election.

10 "J. D. Vance Delivers Republican National Convention Speech," CNN, June 17, 2024, https://transcripts.cnn.com/show/se/date/2024-07-17/segment/04.

13 J. D. Vance, *Hillbilly Elegy: A Memoir of a Family and Culture in Crisis* (New York: Harper, 2016), 13.

13 Vance, 2.

16 Vance, 156–157.

17 Vance, 163.

23 Vance, 202.

25, 27 Mona Charen, "What *Hillbilly Elegy* Reveals About Trump and America," *National Review*, July 28, 2016, https://www.nationalreview.com/2016/07/hillbilly-elegy-jd-vances-new-book-reveals-much-about-trump-america/.

27 Sarah Jones, "J. D. Vance, the False Prophet of Blue America," *New Republic*, November 17, 2016, https://newrepublic.com/article/138717/jd-vance-false-prophet-blue-america.

28 Bess Levin, "Every Terrible Thing J. D. Vance Said About Trump Before Becoming His Running Mate," *Vanity Fair*, July 16, 2024, https://www.vanityfair.com/news/story/terrible-things-jd-vance-said-about-trump-running-mate.

30 Eric McDaniel, "Trump Endorses J. D. Vance, Wading into Ohio's Contentious Republican Senate Primary," NPR, April 15, 2022, https://www.npr.org/2022/0/15/1093148912/trump-endorses-j-d-vance-wading-into-ohios-contentious-republican-senate-primary.

32 "J. D. Vance Delivers Victory Speech After Win in Senate Race," Rev.com, November 8, 2022, https://webflow.rev.com/transcripts/j-d-vance-delivers-victory-speech-after-win-in-senate-race.

37 Rachel Treisman, "J. D. Vance Went Viral for 'Cat Lady' Comments. The Centuries-Old Trope Has a Long Tail," NPR, July 29, 2024, https://www.npr.org/2024/07/29/nx-s1-5055616/jd-vance-childless-cat-lady-history.

39 Stefan Becket, "Read the full VP debate transcript from the Walz-Vance showdown," CBS, October 2, 2024, https://www.cbsnews.com/news/full-vp-debate-transcript-walz-vance-2024.

SELECTED BIBLIOGRAPHY

Gomez, Henry J., and Matt Dixon. "The Inside Story of How Trump Chose J. D. Vance as His Running Mate." NBC News, July 15, 2024. https://www.nbcnews.com/politics/donald-trump/trump-chose-jd-vance-running-mate-vp-pick-rcna161982.

Hillbilly Elegy. IMDb.com, accessed September 25, 2024. https://www.imdb.com/title/tt6772802/.

"J. D. Vance Delivers Republican National Convention Speech." CNN, June 17, 2024. https://transcripts.cnn.com/show/se/date/2024-07-17/segment/04.

"J. D. Vance Delivers Victory Speech After Win in Senate Race." Rev, November 8, 2022. https://webflow.rev.com/transcripts/j-d-vance-delivers-victory-speech-after-win-in-senate-race.

Levin, Bess. "Every Terrible Thing J. D. Vance Said About Trump Before Becoming His Running Mate." *Vanity Fair*, July 16, 2024. https://www.vanityfair.com/news/story/terrible-things-jd-vance-said-about-trump-running-mate.

Smyth, Julie Carr. "What's in a Name? Republican Vice Presidential Nominee J. D. Vance Has Had Many of Them." AP News, updated July 26, 2024. https://apnews.com/article/election-2024-republicans-vice-president-vance-name-359c3d1361c94f5d2d1e9798b7854477.

Vance, J. D. *Hillbilly Elegy: A Memoir of a Family and Culture in Crisis.* New York: Harper, 2016.

LEARN MORE

Britannica Kids: J. D. Vance
https://kids.britannica.com/students/article/JD-Vance/635898

Conaghan, Bernard. *Marine Corps*. New York: Crabtree, 2023.

Finn, Peter. *Electing U.S. Senators*. Buffalo: Cavendish Square, 2025.

Leed, Percy. *Donald Trump, 2nd Edition: Unprecedented Politician*. Minneapolis: Lerner Publications, 2025.

National Geographic Kids: Donald Trump
https://kids.nationalgeographic.com/history/article/donald-trump

National Geographic Kids: What Is the Job of the US President?
https://kids.nationalgeographic.com/history/article/what-is-the-job-of-the-us-president

INDEX

Photo Acknowledgments

Image Credits: AP Photo/Jae C. Hong, p. 2; AP Photo/Julia Nikhinson, p. 6; Jabin Botsford/The Washington Post/Getty Images, p. 8; KAMIL KRZACZYNSKI/AFP/Getty Images, p. 9; Robert Gauthier/Los Angeles Times/Getty Images, p. 10; halbergman/Getty Images, p. 11; Luke Sharrett for The Washington Post/Getty Images, p. 12; Rainer Lesniewski/Shutterstock, p. 14; Wikimedia Commons PD, pp. 17, 21; U.S. Marine Corps photo by Cpl. Sarah M. Grawcock/Alamy, p. 18; pawel.gaul/Getty Images, p. 20; sshepard/Getty Images, p. 22; PRAKASH SINGH/AFP/Getty Images, p. 23; Jeff Swensen/Getty Images, p. 24; Ben Molyneux/Alamy, p. 25; BFA/Alamy, p. 26; MARK RALSTON/AFP/Getty Images, p. 27; Steve Jennings/Getty Images for TechCrunch, p. 29; Drew Angerer/Getty Images, p. 30; Joshua A. Bickel/Bloomberg/Getty Images, p. 31; Megan Jelinger/Bloomberg/Getty Images, p. 32; United States Congress, p. 33; Jabin Botsford/The Washington Post/Getty Images, p. 34; Scott Olson/Getty Images, p. 36; Alex Wong/Getty Images, p. 37; Michele Crowe/CBS/Getty Images, p. 39. Cover: AP Photo/Paul Vernon.